Victoria Sketchbook

Active Pass

Victoria Sketchbook

Robert Amos

ORCA BOOK PUBLISHERS

National Library of Canada Cataloguing in Publication Data

Amos, Robert, 1950 -

Victoria sketchbook

ISBN 1-55143-197-1

1. Victoria (B.C.)- -Guidebooks. 2. Victoria (B.C.)- - Pictorial works. I. Title.

FC3846.18.A46 2002   917.11'28044   C2002-910272 - 3

F1089.5.V6A46 2002

First published in the United States, 2002

Orca Book Publishers gratefully acknowledges the support for its publishing programs provided by the following agencies: the Government of Canada through the Book Publishing Industry Development Program (BPIDP), the Canada Council for the Arts, and the British Columbia Arts Council.

Design: Christine Toller
All illustrations & paintings: Robert Amos
Map: Jim Brennan
Printed and bound in Canada

IN CANADA:
Orca Book Publishers
PO Box 5626, Station B
Victoria, BC Canada
V8R 6S4

IN THE UNITED STATES:
Orca Book Publishers
PO Box 468
Custer, WA USA
98240-0468

04 03 02 • 5 4 3 2 1

for Sarah

Key to map

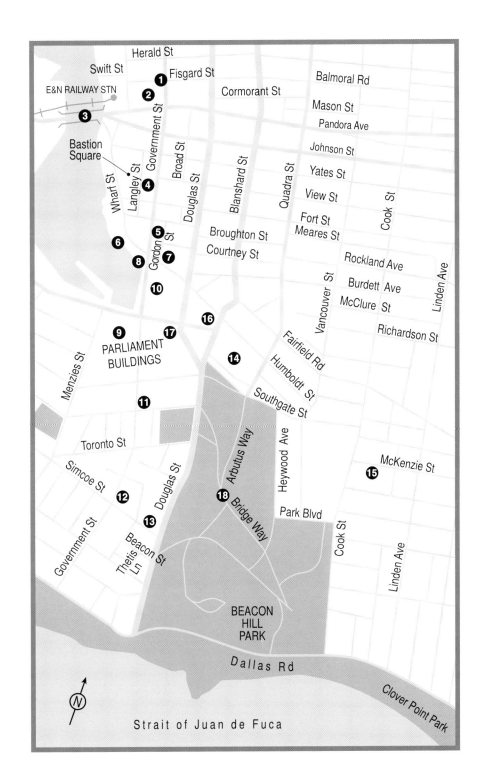

Herald St

Swift St

Fisgard St

❶

❷

E&N RAILWAY STN

Balmoral Rd

Cormorant St

Mason St

Pandora Ave

❸

Johnson St

Bastion
Square

Yates St

View St

Government St

Langley St

Broad St

Blanshard St

Quadra St

Cook St

❹

Whart St

Douglas St

Fort St
Meares St

Broughton St

❺

Gordon St

❻

Courtney St

Rockland Ave

Burdett Ave

McClure St

❼

❽

Linden Ave

❿

Richardson St

Vancouver St

❶❻

❾

❶❼

PARLIAMENT
BUILDINGS

❶❹

Fairfield Rd

Humboldt St

Menzies St

Southgate St

❶❶

Toronto St

Arbutus Way

Heywood Ave

McKenzie St

Simcoe St

❶❺

Douglas St

❶❷

❶❽

Bridge Way

Park Blvd

Government St

❶❸

Beacon St

Cook St

Thetis Ln

Linden Ave

BEACON
HILL
PARK

Dallas Rd

Clover Point Park

N

Strait of Juan de Fuca

Inner Harbour

I REMEMBER the first time I drove into Victoria. The view from the hilltop at Royal Oak brought me up short. There was the city spread below me. Sunlight sparkled on the waters of the Strait of Juan de Fuca, and beyond was a curtain of cobalt blue: the mountains of the Olympic Peninsula. I knew I was going to stay.

Victoria is beautiful, no doubt about it. And beyond that, I found many reasons to stay — the Mediterranean climate, the relaxed attitude, the cultural life spiced with flavours of Olde England, the First Nations of the Pacific Northwest, and the people of the Orient.

I describe Victoria as a city where the feminine is in the ascendant. After all, where else are there baskets of flowers hanging from the lampposts? Most cities seem masculine to me — tall buildings driven ever upward by ambition, boom-and-bust economies characterized by concrete towers topped with revolving restaurants. But Victoria is surrounded by water, and all that vertical energy is moderated. People here are strong on intuition and nurturing. It's a good place for raising children, writing books, and gardening.

How could I make a living in a city without industry, where government and tourism seem to provide the only steady jobs? In desperate need of employment, I applied for work at the Art Gallery of Greater Victoria and was hired, there to spend my days in the world of art. For the next five years, I divided my time between my office upstairs in a big creaking wooden mansion, and the collections stored downstairs in the gallery's basement, hewn from the living rock. There I fed my imagination with the collection of Japanese prints, British watercolours, and the as-yet-unwritten art history of British Columbia.

After working hours, I discovered a landscape that made my heart sing. Walking home, I marvelled at the gardens of Rockland, dense with planting. Along the sidewalk's edge, every nook and rocky crevice overflowed with purple aubretia and nodding Canterbury bells. On the weekends I got on my bicycle and set out to explore.

Victoria is the perfect place for a bicycle. Unlike some cities, where downtown is relentlessly down and going home is an uphill climb, Victoria is a medley of geographical allsorts. Coasting down one little hill, you gain almost enough speed to roll up the next. Because it's at the end of an island, there aren't really any highways to contend with. And between all the bigger roads are networks of sidestreets and byways. Even where it says "no exit," there's almost always a way through for a bicycle.

The fresh salt air of the seashore is never far away. The foghorn moans, and a seagull's cry enlivens the soundscape. Causeways and wharves garland the edge of the Inner Harbour. Further promenades — Dallas Road and the Westsong Way — lead along the water's edge and offer Victorians psychic relief at all hours of day and night. Our eyes embrace the far horizons, and the white noise of lapping waves smooths our ruffled feathers. Every inlet and cove is the focus of a neighbourhood, from Saxe Point through to Willows Beach and on beyond Cordova Bay. Grass or sand or shingling rock leads down to a shoreline that is always public property up to ten feet above the tideline.

The Tourist Information Centre is situated in a landmark art moderne pylon. Built in 1931 as a gas station, it originally had California-style tile roofs over the gas pumps. The tower was topped by a 10-million-candlepower beacon, meant to guide aviators at night. The beacon hasn't been functional in many years, and planes are not allowed to fly into or out of the harbour between dusk and dawn.

Tourist Information Centre

The evening stroll is a Victoria tradition, a constitutional to banish postprandial torpor. Turning away from the water's edge, take the opportunity to consider the homes and gardens of the neighbourhood. Not for us the remote fastness of the gated community or the isolation of the towering high rise. Here, cottages and picket fences are the norm and every garden is a site for self-expression. The best time for a stroll is the "violet hour," that evening moment when lights are turned on inside but the curtains have yet to be drawn. Through other people's windows, life looks so simple, so comfortable, so well-disposed.

Almost all Victoria homes are made of wood, which allows for considerable expression of taste. The gingerbread and finials on the rambling mansions of Rockland mark our skyline. Overhanging eaves of California bungalows are the hallmark of the cozy "arts and crafts" taste. On welcoming porches, wicker furniture beckons beneath the honeysuckle. Recently we have begun to appreciate our city's curvilinear stucco, the geometry of art deco and moderne. Buildings with these clean lines grace some of our scenic viewpoints.

Before 1901, Victoria was divided by James Bay, a narrow inlet which dwindled into a tidal mud flat. But then, for two years, pile drivers thumped day and night, driving 2,953 timber piles down to the bedrock 125 feet below. Each piling is as long as the Empress Hotel is tall. Today, the hotel's wooden foundation is as solid as when it was new, for the wood is kept damp and well-preserved in the water and mud.

The Fairmont Empress Hotel

Ship Point   The Empress   Causeway

The Inner Harbour

Victoria has less than one-fifth of Vancouver's population. Yet it remains the capital of the province. You might wonder why. Perhaps it has something to do with those buildings with the green domes on top. The Parliament Buildings (1897) were designed by Francis Rattenbury, a 25-year-old Yorkshireman, who entered the competition under the nom de plume "B.C. Architect." He did such a wonderful job designing the Parliament Buildings that the capital of this province will never move to the larger and

Carillon   Royal B.C. Museum   The Parliament Buildings

more convenient city of Vancouver. That's the power of architecture. In addition, Rattenbury conceived of and designed the Empress Hotel (1907) and the Crystal Gardens (1925). He also designed the C.P.R. Steamships office (1924), a sort of Greek temple which provides a monumental introduction to the ceremonial tone Rattenbury intended for the Inner Harbour. For many years it has been the home of the Royal London Wax Museum.

The Sunny Side of the Street

Looking up Government Street

Early on, Victoria decided it didn't want its sightlines interrupted by tall buildings. The few that were built — some as tall as twelve storeys! — stand in mute reproach. To counter vertical density and urban sprawl, Victoria has chosen "in-fill" as a strategy. Houses are continually being added to or lifted into the air to create a new ground-floor suite. It's always interesting to see what goes on behind the hedges.

Victorians are said to be perenially fifteen years behind the times and seem determined to stay that way. Every sort of advance, progress, or development is met with an almost insurmountable inertia. We sit secure behind our defenses with a "drawbridge mentality." Everything was perfect at the moment we arrived and would remain so if we could just raise the drawbridge and retire into our island fastness.

Some people imagine it's boring in Victoria. The choice of diversion is certainly not as broad as what's on offer in the megalopolis. But, surprisingly, our cultural life is full. Victoria is a mecca for creative people, who come to live or visit here. Art galleries, museums, opera, authors — there is always something of world class going on, though usually just one thing at a time. And because there's just one, you really feel you ought to attend.

Architect Thomas Hooper endeared himself to Victorians by designing the fragrant shop of Rogers' Chocolates on Government Street. Built in 1893, it shows an Arts and Crafts style.

Rogers' Chocolates

Moreover, culture is incredibly accessible in Victoria. If you can't walk to it, you'll find parking is easy and line-ups are never long. What sells out in the big cities is poorly attended here, where the pleasure of staying at home is a force to be reckoned with.

This is a small town, but a small town of a different sort. Demographically, the population is cosmopolitan, well-educated, and wealthy — in a coupon-clipping, fixed-income sort of way. Many have taken early retirement, chosen "quality of life," and arrived here with abundant life-experience and good ideas about how to fill their time.

In the early days, Victoria was a perfect haven for colonial administrators. Faced with precarious health in the pestilential back-waters of a South Asian outpost or a return to the dull weather and bland food of grey old England, they were pleased to settle on these Pacific shores. Here was a surprisingly familiar landscape, a benevolent climate, and an Anglo culture free from the worst aspects of the class structure they left behind.

Victoria is the home of some pretty advanced anti-smoking bylaws. Ironically, Morris Tobacconists (1892) is one of the city's best-loved shops. Designed by Thomas Hooper in a handsome art nouveau style, the store is outfitted with onyx and mahogany, and redolent of the aroma of pipe tobacco.

Morris Tobacconists

On May 24 every year, Victoria celebrates Queen Victoria's birthday. To mark the occasion, a huge parade comes down Douglas Street. As well as all the local Shriners, dozens of American high-school marching bands pile out of buses and take over the town. They are here strutting their stuff, hoping for a place in the Rosebowl Parade in Pasadena, California.

The Union Club

Now it is the retired university presidents, diplomats, authors, and art collectors who choose this refuge. Behind the hedges, many Victorians nurture their creative souls. Newcomers may experience moments of tedium. Then come the things one always intended to do — if one ever had the time. Slowly, self-directed projects begin to take shape — memoir writing, fine woodworking, the pursuit of watercolour painting or playing the flute. And with these preoccupations comes an awareness of the many others quietly pursuing their own interests.

Victoria is situated on a low-lying promontory, and the weather sweeps by it, fresh and full of vigour after a 5,000-mile voyage across the Pacific. Fresh air is one of the things I like best about Victoria.

In some cities the mountains have moved considerably up-stage — a towering, hovering presence. But in Victoria the mountains stay at a respectful distance. The horizon in Victoria is very horizontal. It looks like an easy place to live.

In 1897, gold seekers lined up in front of the old Customs House (built 1876). Victoria was the only place to get a licence to prospect in the Klondike. The prospectors might or might not find gold, but the merchants of Victoria certainly lined their own pockets with silver during the first Fraser gold rush (1858), subsequent finds in the Cariboo (early 1860s) and then in the Yukon (1897).

Thunderbird Park

Mungo Martin was a Kwakwaka'wakw native who grew up at Fort Rupert on the north end of this island. In 1952 he was invited to Victoria by the government to carve replicas of old totem poles. Thought to be the last carver of his "dying race," in fact he came to teach a new generation. Martin built his ancestral community house amid the totems in Thunderbird Park (1953). Adjacent to the Royal B.C. Museum, this has been a centrepiece for the renaissance of proud First Nations cultures.

Victoria is a tourist town — no getting away from that. In fact, why would you want to? As soon as I discovered it, I decided to settle in. But a certain feeling of curiosity, of openness to the wonders and contradictions of this place, has never left me. For almost thirty years I've been living here, painting pictures of every part of Victoria, and writing about Victorians in the Victoria newspaper. And I still feel like a tourist, a voyeur, a discoverer of unanticipated felicities. "Be a tourist in your own town" is a spring tradition in Victoria, and for me the feeling never stops.

We really are a bit of the end of the British Empire, aren't we? The old cup of tea, tweed curtain clipped moustache sort of thing. Private schools, cricket, regimental honours hanging in the Cathedral. Here the Monarchist League and the Daughters of the British Empire soldier on. But there is a playfulness and humour that make Victoria a nonstop costume party. One can only be a genuine eccentric in a place where there is so much tradition, even if it is borrowed tradition.

The Church of Our Lord (1874) was the result of a theological dispute. Reverend Edward Cridge, once Dean of Christ Church Cathedral, seceded with 250 of his parishioners and formed this Reformed Episcopal Church. This board-and-batten, "carpenter gothic" style church conveys a rustic piety, in contrast to the stone and cement Cathedral up on the hill.

The Church of Our Lord

St. Ann's Academy was a Roman Catholic school for girls and the convent of the Sisters of St. Ann. The sisters moved away in 1974, and after much debate the Provincial Capital Commission renovated the building in 1997. The jewel of the project was the restoration of the chapel. The delightful Quebecois baroque chapel (1858) originally stood on a site across the road. It was hauled on skids to the Academy grounds and attached to St. Ann's in 1886. Though no longer a consecrated church, St. Ann's is popular as a wedding venue.

St. Ann's Academy

31

The Johnson Street Bridge (1924) was designed by the Strauss Bascule Bridge Company of San Francisco (which also designed the Golden Gate Bridge). As well as having a roadway and a bike path, this cantilever bridge has a separate deck for the railway.

Victoria Harbour Ferry

Victoria has the original Chinese community in Canada. At first settled by gold seekers and the men who built the railways, Victoria's Chinatown was second only to San Francisco's during the nineteenth century. Its importance dwindled as years went by.

The Gate of Harmonious Interest (1981) is the centrepiece of a revived Chinatown. Called Tong Ji Men in Chinese, it is huge and authentic in every detail. After some years, rain and frost damaged the original made-in-Taiwan ceramic roof tiles and ornamental figures. They were replaced in 1997 with perfect replicas made in Victoria.

The Chinese Public School (1908) is the most oriental building in Chinatown. It was not designed by a Chinese architect but by D.C. Frame, who went on to design the Memorial Arena (1946). The school is the pagoda-like structure on the right in the painting. It is fitted out with classical brackets under the eaves, Gothic trefoil fretwork on the balconies, Moorish windows on the first floor, and Italianate window heads.

The school was created in reaction to racist laws, which kept Chinese-born children from attending regular schools. Those laws were overturned and, ever since, the school has been used to teach Chinese language and culture. Two hundred and fifty children attend classes here every day after regular school and for half a day on Saturday. The school folk-dance troupe is frequently called upon to welcome dignitaries with their "Junior Lion Dancers."

Fisgard Street

Fan Tan Alley

Lion Dance

Craigdarroch Castle (1890) isn't really a castle. It is a monster house, built on the highest point of land in the Scottish baronial style. Robert Dunsmuir, who built Craigdarroch, developed coal mines at Nanaimo and built a railroad to take the coal to the Royal Navy at Esquimalt. Dunsmuir was building this home to impress his peers, the railroad barons who were building their own "castles" on Knob Hill in San Francisco.

Dunsmuir died before it was finished, leaving his widow, three unmarried daughters, and some orphaned grandchildren to move in. Though Joan Dunsmuir was the wealthiest woman in Canada, the castle may have been a little lonely. The family lived there until 1910, when the property was subdivided.

Buyers purchased lots by raffle, and one ticket holder won the castle. Before long, it reverted to the city for taxes and began its career as a college and a music school.

Craigdarroch has now been restored to something like – or beyond – its former glory by the Craigdarroch Museum Society. Decoration of the rooms with period furnishings is an ongoing project. Craigdarroch is a very popular tourist attraction, and its success has enabled the entire fabric of the building – from the masonry of the basement to the red slate roof – to be brought up to standards which would make Robert Dunsmuir proud.

Craigdarroch Castle

The Bird Cages Confectionary

This cute little shop, across the street from the Parliament Buildings, is called the Bird Cages Confectionary. Victoria's first Legislature was called The Birdcages in jest by the locals, for the buildings were thought to resemble a group of birdcages or Chinese pagodas.

Emily Carr (1871 - 1945), author and artist, had this small apartment building constructed on her portion of her parents' property. Since then it has become legendary as the site of her book, The House of All Sorts.

Carr was ignored in her time, but has since become one of Canada's most famous painters. At the time of her death she left her best paintings and the proceeds from her estate to the people of British Columbia as the Emily Carr Trust Collection. These paintings were taken to Vancouver and eventually became the property of the Vancouver Art Gallery. The Art Gallery of Greater Victoria has a smaller collection, which is often on view. The largest collection of Carr's work is stored in Victoria at the British Columbia Archives.

Emily Carr is Canada's most important artist. During her long and productive life she gave her attention to the great themes of our times in paint and in words.

She was a woman who knew she had to do it on her own, at a time when women were defined by the men who kept them. But married life would have compromised her creativity. She gave her life to art.

Helped by her Native friends, Carr discovered that the First Nations people here had a deeply satisfying way of living in this place, at a time when the government was working to erase their culture.

Carr felt the life force moving in the trees and believed it was worthy of worship. The conservation movement has grown since her time, but her message remains the same.

The goal of Emily Carr, as an artist, was a sort of transcendence. She sensed that life was moved by a spirit larger than herself. She prepared, through a life of rigorous training, to discover and respond to the spirit of every transcendent moment.

207 Government Street, The Birthplace of Emily Carr

Medieval Bridge, Beacon Hill Park

Circle Drive, Beacon Hill Park

So how can we describe Victoria? This little city by the sea has been caught in an identity crisis for many years. Clearly the days of "more English than the English" have gone, leaving a veneer of mock-Tudor architecture and tea at the Empress. The flavours of old Chinatown have been co-opted and gentrified by artists and lawyers. Lumbering and fishing, which were the economic backbone of the region, aren't what they used to be.

Pilot Street at Dallas Road

Pilot Street, lined with salt-bleached cottages, runs a few blocks down to the seaside. This is a land of lawn chairs and herbaceous borders. A solitary lawn mower purrs along under the dark red leaves of boulevard trees. At the beach close by, seagulls screech; sea lions bark offshore and occasionally a pod of orcas passes in the distance. The little red pilot boat leaves Ogden Point to meet a passing freighter and, in the distance, sunshine sparkles off the water. I lift up my eyes to the snowcapped peaks of the Olympic Peninsula, and my spirit is refreshed. This is the essence of Victoria.

Broom, Dallas Road

I created this *Victoria Sketchbook* so you could share the pleasure I find in this city that I love. The pictures are all watercolours and are reproduced actual size. The locations are within easy walking distance of one another. So take this book in hand and join me, discovering a beautiful city by the sea.